Teenagers, Employee Engagement and What You Can Learn

"6 facts that transcend employee engagement"

Richard Conde

**To everyone I have worked with who has
made me a better leader**

Contents

Teenagers, Employee Engagement and What You Can Learn

Introduction

I don't know about you, but wherever I go it seems most employees are not happy at work. I generally talk to employees of any business I happen to visit. Collectively, the general theme I hear from employees is: 1) how ready they are to leave work, 2) how they want to be somewhere else, and 3) how unhappy they are. If you are anything like me, you've had similar experiences. Most statistics sadly point out that 70% of employees are actively disengaged at work. What that means to me is 7 out of 10 employees are merely going through the motions while at work, not adding any real value to the business. As you can imagine, this negatively impacts the business' bottom line, plus it increases employee turnover, a major expense for most organizations.

Increasing employee engagement is a big challenge for today's leaders. This enigma does not merely lie at the feet of Human Resources, but is the responsibility of every leader within an organization. Before we further explore employee engagement, let's start by defining it. So what is employee engagement? For me, the answer is rather simple.   Employee engagement is the willingness of an employee to choose to go above and beyond their normal everyday tasks.

When an employee chooses to do "more", s/he is telling you they are buying into the corporate culture, are aligned with the leader's vision and have taken ownership of the business. There are reams of data which quantify the differences between an engaged employee and a disengaged employee. The differences can be measured by comparing such things as productivity, absenteeism, involvement, idea generation, turnover, etc.

When I became involved in the fast casual food industry, I quickly realized the value of employee engagement as it related to service, absenteeism, employee turnover and shrinkage (product as well as profits). Quite simply, my personal financial success lied in the hands of teenagers who easily go from one job to another without regard. With turnover in the fast casual food industry at 50%, I had to figure something out. If I did not engage my employees at a different level, the cost of training new employees and lost productivity would cause me to close the doors.

This book will cover the techniques I used to increase employee engagement which proved to be rather successful. From a measurable stand point, I was able to decrease turnover below 10% and virtually eliminate absenteeism. In addition, there was an increase in teamwork, employee involvement, store cleanliness, generation of ideas and most importantly, customer service.

The next six facts will outline the tactics I used with a group of diverse Gen-Y employees that you can easily utilize with all your employees to build a more engaged, dynamic and productive work force.

Fact #1 – PEOPLE ARE PEOPLE

During my countless interaction with people from different walks of life, I have found we have more in common than not. It starts with the fact we are all part of the human race. All of our needs have the same basic hierarchical importance. Maslow figured this out long ago when he created "Maslow's Human Hierarchy of Needs". Just as a reminder, below is Maslow's model.

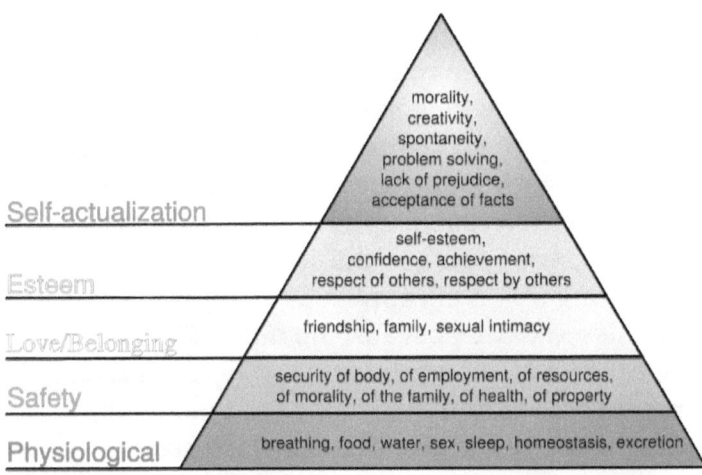

I would argue that the more you are able to have an employee experience the different levels of Maslow's hierarchy of needs, the greater their engagement in the business. Optimally, if an employee is able to self-actualize with the job, it will lead to the greatest employee engagement possible. So, how does it all start?

1 – Hire the right person

It starts with bringing in employees that match your company culture. A mistake I made early on was looking for and hiring employees who possessed only functional skills that I could 'plug and play'. I recall one of my first hires was a lady by the name of Stacey. Stacey had solid experience and knowledge of the fast casual food industry. After going through the interview process, I hired Stacey. From my perspective, it was a no brainer. We had a need for "x" expertise, Stacy had "x" experience, it was a natural fit. At the same time, there was a need to hire an employee to open the store during the weekends. A young man by the name of Carlos stopped by the store asking if we were hiring, one of the other employees told him yes, so Carlos completed an application. In the next two weeks, Carlos came to the store four times, following up on his application. At first, I dismissed Carlos because he did not have the right level of experience. But, due to his perseverance and demeanor I felt he would fit the company culture. Fast forward six months, Carlos had been promoted to shift leader, while Stacey was no longer employed. My learning was simple; **I put too much emphasis on functional knowledge**. I quickly evolved and began looking for two important qualities: 1) Will the employee fit the culture? 2) Has the employee demonstrated the willingness to learn? If they have, <u>trust me, they will learn</u>. This may sound a bit remedial but, **believe it or not, people are able to learn new things**. I do not know anyone who was born with the knowledge they will have when they die. Life is a journey and, as people, we love to learn and grow (Self Actualization).

If you put more weight on someone's functional knowledge than their ability to learn, you focus on the 'now' rather than the employee's potential. If an employee does not fit your corporate culture, s/he will always have an internal emptiness, much like **you trying to put a square peg in a round hole.** Last time I checked, a square peg doesn't fit a round hole.

After what I learned from hiring Stacey, my hiring practices changed. I focused on making sure the candidate would fit our culture and that they had a strong desire to learn. Once I began focusing on these two areas, **I hired a large number of employees who spent multiple years** working at the stores and formed the basis for a turnover rate below 10%.

2 – Birds of a feather flock together

There is something about Gen-Y employees (I believe all employees) who enjoy working with friends or people they know. I realize many employees are hesitant hiring people who know each other, who are friends or relatives, but my experience was the opposite. **Good employees refer other good employees.** The funny thing is, if top employees fit your culture, more than likely their friends will have similar interests which will also, more than likely, be in agreement with your corporate culture. Carlos referred Tihuy who referred Moreland. Vince referred Blanca who referred Jose. Each of these employees lasted multiple years in the stores. Similarly, there were countless other referrals who lasted multiple years. Very rarely do you see, in the fast casual food industry, an employee lasting multiple years, much less several employees.

By having "friends" working together it benefited the business in many ways. For example: 1) People like being around people with whom they have things in common. There is a greater spirit of kinship, 2) the referral process builds accountability for both parties. The person who referred the employee does not want to tarnish their reputation while the person who was referred does not want to let their friend down, 3) training is facilitated since there is a more meaningful exchange between the two parties, and 4) it creates a sense of teamwork quickly and efficiently. So now it's your turn. **Your employees should be your best recruiters**. Reach out to them and have them be your champion. Encourage each employee to refer at least one person per quarter. Keep in mind, if

ALL their referrals fall short, are not considered or interviewed, or are not hired, they will stop referring, which could lead to potential disengagement. By the way, if your employees are not your biggest advocates or their referrals are abysmal, it means they are **NOT** engaged.

Read on. By the time you finish this book and implement the outlined steps, you will have some true and tested tactics that will allow you to increase employee engagement.

3 – Say goodbye the right way

There are times when things don't work out, that's life. This is exemplified by the number of exchanges at department stores, the number of individuals that are let go from work each year, etc. **It's not the 'what' but the 'how'**. By no means can you, or anyone, tolerate bad performance. No business can thrive on employees performing poorly. But you can handle the communication multiple ways. Whichever way you choose has consequences, some positive, others negative.

I wanted for all my employees to boast about the stores and speak positively about the product and brand. With the onset of social media, it is easy for a disgruntled employee to eradicate your reputation with a simple post on Facebook or a tweet. Therefore, I made sure to treat all employees with respect, **not just the good**

employees. I recall an employee by the name of Teresa. Teresa was an employee that was inherited from the previous regime. Teresa had a lot of skill, but little will. After realizing Teresa was consistently falling short of her duties, she was placed on a performance plan. Unfortunately, she quickly moved through the performance plan to be terminated. When Teresa and I met, I could have done it one of two ways. I could have pointed out her mistakes and simply fired her, or I could allow her to own her behavior and realize we were parting ways.

Even though the second option took more time to complete, in the end, Teresa acknowledged her mistakes, agreed she had not held up her end of the bargain and accepted accountability for her dismissal. Teresa's story does not end there. After ending her employment, she became a customer, a rather good customer, stopping by at least once a week. She also told the existing employees **how fortunate they were to be working for me.** You see, Teresa went to work somewhere else, where people were **NOT** treated like people. She was just a number, just an employee. Teresa became a testament of our employee engagement. She positively impacted the existing staff because she was treated with respect!!!!

Fact #2 – KNOW WHEN TO HOLD THEM; WHEN TO FOLD THEM

It is crucial to set the right tone early, establish the culture, set the guidelines of what is permissible and allow the employees to understand the boundaries. Equally as important is the ability for the employee to understand the business, how it functions and how they fit into the success of the business. **When the employee succeeds, the business wins**. Many times, most employees perform their day functions without understanding how they affect the bottom line.

1-Start strong, let go as needed

As a leader, you are always inheriting a situation. Whether it's a brand new position or following a prior leader, there is always "baggage" that remains. I once read "The Heart of a Leader" by Ken Blanchard. In his book, Mr. Blanchard made the point that, as a leader, is it easier to come in strong and loosen up than to come in loose and then tighten up. I learned as I became involved with the stores, the importance of setting the right tone early. I held an initial meeting with all personnel explaining: 1) My background 2) My expectations 3) My standards 4) My style 5) My "hot buttons". Moreover, and more importantly, I asked them about: 1) Their background 2) Their expectations 3) Their standards 4) Their style 5) Their "hot buttons". During this conversation, **as a group, we agreed on how we were going to move forward**. Each side clearly understanding what each expected from the other.

Similar to any relationship, there are times when one side lets the other down. **During these times it is important to express ones feelings, let the other party know of the issue and hold them accountable**. In the fast casual food industry, it is important that the trash in the lobby area is discarded timely throughout the day. One of my "hot buttons" was timely disposal of trash. On a specific instance, I visited the store and noticed the trash in the lobby nearly overflowing. I immediately spoke with the shift leader on hand, Gabriel. I asked Gabriel to explain to me the requirements of clearing out the trash in the lobby. Gabriel immediately explained the policy, outlining the schedule to check and clear the trash. He even mentioned this was one of my hot buttons. When I asked why the trash was not taken out, he did not have a valid explanation. We discussed the consequences of his action, reiterated the expectation and secured additional agreement from him. After our stern conversation, there wasn't an additional time where Gabriel did not timely monitor and take out the trash. In my experience, people who report to you want to follow a strong leader. **Employees respect a person who not only talks the talk but also walks the walk.**

2 – A free coke equals $3,000

Most employees in a business do not understand the cost of running a business, what it takes to be profitable and how the small things add up. In the fast casual food business you quickly learn how pennies add up to dollars. During the initial meeting with the inherited employees, it was critical for each to understand the business. Part of my initial meeting with the employees was to explain the store's profit and loss statement. In a fun way, I explained: 1) what were the drivers of profitability, and 2) how each employee affected the bottom line. For example, during my initial meeting with a new or existing employee, I would ask "What is the retail price for a soft drink?" They would answer accordingly. I would then ask "how much would it cost **US (not me)** if each employee gave away a free drink once a week?" They would answer accordingly. Then, I would ask them to multiply it times 52 weeks. The number could be staggering; depending on the product, giving away a free drink would impact the business by $3,000 annually. Lastly, I would ask them what would happen if their parents, or if they, had to give up $3,000 every year. Although the answers varied, they all agreed it would be devastating. I was able to tie how their performance would impact the bottom line. Each employee knew the cost and profit margin associated with each product. In fact, **they were so aware of the business, they could tell you the expense of a cup, spoons, the electric bill, etc.**

On a monthly basis, I would share the Profit and Loss statement with all employees. They knew exactly how the business was doing and what was positively or negatively impacting profit. By being transparent, **each employee became vested in the overall success of the operation**.

3 – Is that the stanky legg or the Ricky Bobby

What culture do you want to create? For me it was simple. Work hard and have fun. **It is important to not hold yourself at a higher standard than your direct reports**. When the stores were busy, all hands on deck. When it was slow, fun would be had by all. I remember a specific time when the crew decided to go to the back of the store and have a dance contest. They turned the music up and they took turns doing the Stanky Legg, the Ricky Bobby and a couple of other dances. I sponsored the event by being the judge and giving the winner a gift certificate. What amazed me the most about that day was the fact that as soon as customers started coming into the store, everyone quickly focused on providing extraordinary service. The music volume was decreased, all employees took their positions in the front of the store and the focus was on the business. Each crew member was keenly aware of their expectations, but also knew they were seen as humans who treasured friendships (Maslow's Love/Belonging). **A leader needs to always make sure the culture is consistent.** This creates comfort and consistency among employees.

4 – Be true to your word

As a leader, it is critical to stand behind your words. If you say you are going to do something, do it. One of the principles I set in place was rewarding employees for making an A on their report card. If the report card had all 'A's", the bounty was multiplied. In addition, for any employee in college, I would reimburse their tuition if a certain GPA was met. During his third year at the store, Vince was going to a local college. I made the agreement with him that if he reached a certain GPA, I would reimburse the cost of his tuition. In December of that year, Vince called me with the good news. He completed his first semester in college and exceeded the GPA we agreed upon. I was excited and happy for Vince, but at the same time, it was a financially difficult time for the business. However, **I made a promise to Vince and had to stand behind it.** As promised, I reimbursed

Vince for his tuition. As a leader, if you say you are going to do something, <u>the only choice you have is to do it.</u> **You are only as good as your word**. By keeping my commitment, it bought more loyalty from Vince than I could have ever hoped to have. By following through as I promised, I noticed how Vince became a pseudo owner. He became the eyes and ears when I was not around. All of this without me having to formally ask Vince to 'step up". He simply chose to be more involved with all aspects of the store.

Fact #3 – YOUR MOTHER IS FROM AFRICA, YOUR DAD IS IN CHINA

What do you know about your employees? What do you know about their families? What do they know about you? How can you lead someone you know nothing about? In my experience, **there isn't anything more important than getting to know your employees**. This does not mean go out and have a relationship outside of work. But it does mean **you should understand all your employees at a human level**: 1) What is their passion 2) What is important to them 3) Where were they born 4) What was their life journey. These are some basic things you should know about your employees. If you are not able to connect at a human level, you will **NEVER** be able to fully engage them.

1 – What do your parents do for a living?

Having mostly teenage employees, it was important to me to meet the parents of all of them. Also, it was crucial to have a friendly relationship with their parents. This **allowed me to better understand my employee, where they came from and help foresee any potential issues**. For example, Blanca had two sisters and lived in a single parent household. Her mother worked two jobs to provide for her family. By knowing a little about Blanca's home life, **I was able to work with her schedule**, be prepared that Saturdays could be stressful as those were the days her mother worked virtually two jobs. **My understanding of Blanca went from just that of an employee, to more of a human being that has challenges, good and bad times (like all of us)**. If I had not taken time to know her family, her challenges and struggles, I would have never been able to fully engage Blanca, the employee, the person, the human being. By the way, Blanca worked in the stores for over 3 years. That type of employee loyalty is difficult to find these days. The main reason for poor employee engagement is the **leader's inability to connect with their employee on a human to human level**.

2 – Football, basketball, volleyball, homework???

What is important in the life of your employee? DO YOU KNOW!! I would say most leaders do not take time to know what is important for each of their employees. But just knowing is not enough. You should take time to participate, be part of what is important to them.

Blanca played varsity volleyball for her high school team. She loved volleyball. In fact, she would talk about it all the time. One day I asked her to provide me with her team's volleyball schedule. At first, she was surprised I cared enough to find out when she played, not to mention her disbelief that **I would actually show up.** One evening, my wife and I drove 30 minutes to attend Blanca's volleyball game. We sat next to Blanca's mother during the game. When Blanca saw us at the game, her face lit up. **She realized I cared for her beyond that of an employee**. The funny thing was, after I watched Blanca at her game, she became an even better employee. She would update me on the store's activities. She would keep the manager "honest" by pointing ways he could minimize product expenses. For months after we attended her game, **Blanca talked about how much it meant for us to attend her game.** Did I mention Blanca was part of our team for over three years?

Similarly, we watched Carlos play a starting position for his football team on numerous occasions. If you recall, Carlos was key in referring top employees and worked for us for nearly 3 years as well. Moreover, we watched Andy lead his basketball team to many victories. He worked for us for nearly two years. Andy, on multiple occasions, thanked us for taking the time to watch him play basketball. Similar to Blanca, **Andy became a more engaged employee** when he understood he was not a number or an employee but something more valuable and important, **A HUMAN!!**

Attending a game may seem fun and not much of a sacrifice for a leader. After all, athletic events are exciting and the food at the games can be tasty, but it took time and effort. There was the case of Tihuy, who was extremely focused on his academics. I recall a story shared once with me about Tihuy. Apparently at some point Tihuy was part of the football team. He was not very good at football, so he did not get to play much. During a game, Tihuy sat at the end of the bench reading a book that was part of his homework. To me, this illustrated how dedicated Tihuy was to his academics. One day, Tihuy brought his books to work. I asked him what was going on and he told me about an upcoming test the next day. I asked him if I could quiz him to see how ready he was for the test. After a few questions, I realized Tihuy was not ready for his test. So, I told Tihuy to gather his books and go home to study. In addition, I told him not to worry about his shift, that **I would cover it and would make sure he was compensated as normal**. Tihuy asked me, "You are going to pay me to study?" I said "Yes". He was shocked, originally thinking that I was joking. But I was not. So, Tihuy went home, studied and made an A on his test. I always made sure Tihuy continued his focus on his studies. Needless to say, Tihuy became one of the best employees. He worked extra when needed. **He watched the business like his own. He treated customers like his livelihood depended on it**. Day in and day out, customers would complement Tihuy for the outstanding service he provided everyone.

3 – Please don't call me

I am of a certain age where I actually believe a telephone is used for making calls. Imaging that!!! Unfortunately, there is a certain percentage of society who would rather text, Facebook or use Twitter, than have a voice to voice conversation. **The percentage of people who would rather text than talk is growing**.

After being involved with the stores for 4-6 months, establishing the right culture and minimizing employee turnover, **I began to establish solid relationships with my employees**. I was surprised one day when Copeland was at least 30 minutes late for work. When he arrived at the store, I was steaming. One thing employees knew was the importance of being timely. I promptly asked Copeland to the office. He looked a little puzzled why he was in the office. I asked him if he was aware of our notification policy. **He said yes, that is why he sent me a text letting me know football practice lasted longer than anticipated and he would be late.**

I picked up my phone, which had been in the office most of the day, to check for Copeland's text. Sure enough, his text had arrived as he had described. **I immediately thanked Copeland**

for updating me and apologized for not checking my phone.

After this conversation, I realized the policy I had established, where employees had to call me to notify me of any issues, was antiquated. **The policy worked for me, but it did not work for any of my staff members**. I spent the next couple of weeks talking to the employees, asking them if they would prefer to text or talk. The resounding responses were "Don't call me, just text me". I also learned that most, if not all, had Facebook accounts.

This information led me to change my best practices to accommodate my employees. Any communication to be had was done through text. I set up a Facebook page where I would exchange information with the employees. In fact, if there were any operational changes, **I would provide updates through text and Facebook**. In addition, I would use text messages while the employees were working to provide any updates or information. It provided me an instant way to share information.

What I found was a more involved and engaged staff. My employees' feedback allowed me to update a rule that benefited me and only me. **Moreover, the communication regarding procedures was maximized because I was able to communicate it in multiple ways and in ways that the recipient (employee) would prefer and would actually read it**.

I could share many more stories about how I intently got to know each of my employees. Whether it was helping one of their parents find employment, providing a small loan to cover unexpected expenses or provide reference letters on each occasion, **it was about putting the interest of the employee before my personal interest**.

How much time have you spent really getting to know your employee? Once you know more about your employee, have you taken active steps to show you care by supporting them outside of work? If your employee has a hobby, have you attended their event? Have you attended their kids sporting event? **There are many ways of showing support.** You just need to find a few. Trust me they are out there. About this time most people say, "You cannot cross business and personal relationships". I agree; one has to be careful to maintain proper relationships with all co-workers and direct reports. I would add though, it depends on how you approach it. If a leader attends a subordinate's event, acknowledges the employees efforts and shows support, the intent is well received. **The point of attending the event is to show you care for the employee as a person.** You care for them holistically not just for what they do at work.

If we go back to Maslow's Hierarchy, this type of support touches an employee on the Love/Belonging and Esteem levels. **Remember, the higher you can reach an employee on**

Maslow's Hierarchy, the more engaged they will be as an employee.

Fact #4 – GIFT CARD, DECORATE CAKES OR BOTH

What motivates employees? **Most people tend to believe money is the single most motivating factor for employees**. The data shows otherwise. Generally money is further down the list. With that being said, I find that most companies focus on monetary means to motivate employees. **The fact is, most people I know personally admit they would work in a job doing what they love for a decrease in compensation**. How do you determine what motivates employees? **ASK YOUR EMPLOYEES**. Imagine the concept of actually having meaningful conversations with your employees. Many leaders tend to shy away from having open dialogue with their employees based on the employee's terms.

1 – I want to do more

I am continually amazed at the ability of all people to learn and grow, **especially the Gen-Y**

group. The fast casual restaurant business has many simple tasks that need to be completed each day. Each is important in its own right, but none are "sexy". As I mentioned earlier, **it is crucial all employees know how each task they do fits into the big picture**. Part of the training each employee received at the stores was explaining to s/he why each task they completed was important and how it led to a different part of the business. At the end of the training, the employee understood how each task fed other tasks and how individual tasks were part of the big picture.

Additionally, each employee understood what it took to get to the next level. Yep, even in the fast casual restaurant business, it is crucial for employees to have a career path. Without a career path, employees have nothing to strive for. Hence, they become disenchanted and will become interested in a competitor who promises growth opportunities. Everyone came in as a crew member. Of all the employees who were hired, not one, zero, were happy just being a crew member. **All wanted to do something more meaningful and challenging**.

Therefore, it was critical to have a career path for all employees. On the surface, they may not appear as grand opportunities, but they gave each employee a reason to strive for more. One of the more luxurious tasks at the stores was that of cake decorator. Because many customers ordered cakes for special events, this position was highly visible and coveted. The reputation of the store and the likelihood of repeat business many times lied in the quality of the cake decoration. We delegated one main person be the lead cake decorator, **but, like in any other business, it is important that we had backups trained to do multiple tasks**.

Due to the complexity and visibility of the cake decorator role, it was deemed a very important position in the store. As two of my better employees progressed from Crew Member to Senior Crew Member to Shift Leader, they both asked to be trained as cake decorators. At first, I was a little hesitant. I had never envisioned Carolos or Vince in that role. **But, they had both requested the opportunity and both had demonstrated their ability to learn and grow**. We trained Carlos and Vince on how to decorate cakes. Boy, was I glad they were trained. Soon after, my lead cake decorator moved to a job in her chosen degree. Carlos and Vince became lead cake decorators which allowed them to increase their earnings and, at the same time, allowed them to increase their skill set.

I found that employees generally raise their hand for additional opportunities when they are ready for the challenge. **Very rarely do employees ask to move forward if they have not been successful at their current level**. Carlos and Vince, being top performers, were ready for new challenges. Challenges that would keep them more engaged, increase their self-worth and add value to the business. All of these three areas positively affect an employee's Self-

Actualization, which is the highest principle in Maslow's hierarchy.

How many times as a leader have you determined if your staff is ready for the next challenge based on some outdated rule? I often hear leaders say, "A person must be in a job X amount of time before they can move on". I ask, why? Carlos and Vince consistently demonstrated the ability to grow, learn and complete tasks extremely well. If I had not given them the chance to continue their growth by being cake decorators, **they would have thought there wasn't anything left to do;** hence, creating the potential where both would start losing engagement and start looking at outside job opportunities for fulfillment.

2 – Can I please mop!!!!!

Do you know what your employees do well? **Most importantly, do you know what they would prefer to do**? I find that most employees are placed into positions based on what their leader deems they are able to do. This is why I believe a good number of people get into management. Generally, management opportunities give employees the means to move up the corporate ladder and increase their income. **When, in reality, many individuals would rather migrate from leadership positions to do something else. Unfortunately, many companies do not**

present opportunities outside of management for leaders to follow with the same potential for growth.

Richard was an employee who would prefer to be in the back all day cleaning, organizing and putting things away. **He did not enjoy the public interaction of the job**. Kelsey loved talking to customers; **she was exceptional at up selling and relating to our customers.** But Kelsey, hated being away from customers, being in the back was a punishment for her. I asked each of them, individually, if they could develop their ideal job, what it would be. Richard stated he would love to stay in the back, while Kelsey indicated she wanted to deal with customers, exclusively. **Based on their feedback**, we scheduled the two together to allow each to do what they preferred.

A month or so after Richard and Kelsey had been working together, **Kelsey came to me and said**, "The customers I speak with said they would like to see the following specials.......". A day or so later **Richard came to** me and said "I think we can close faster if we do........". **I was astonished with their ideas**. I made Kelsey responsible for coming up with our in store promotions. Similarly, we adopted Richard's ideas across all stores which in turned saved us money because we were closing the stores faster than in the past (reduced labor cost).

By aligning Kelsey's and Richard's strengths to their preferred job function, the business benefited by reducing costs and providing in store promotions that were valuable to our customers. **It is key to be open to your employees' desires**. A hard line rule can cause an employee to feel unimportant. Many years ago, I heard a saying that has been valuable to me **"Put aces in their places"**. By reaching out to your employees, talking to them, listening to their input and implementing their ideas, **you will unearth a polarity between work and their desire that will take employee engagement to the next level**.

3 – No more gift certificates please

In addition to challenging opportunities to build skills and grow as a person, employees need to be recognized for their efforts. As a business, there are special areas of concentration you may want to promote through specific incentive. Or, you may simply want to acknowledge an employee exceeding a goal or going above the call of duty. **Finding the correct incentive that will generate the desired behavior is critical**. Too often, incentives are devised based on what the leader finds valuable or **the metric that is part of the leader's bonus**, rather than what will actually motivate an employee.

In the stores, we had daily sales goals we needed to reach. **As mentioned earlier, the employees knew what the daily break even number was for their store**; therefore, they understood the need to exceed the required goal. Rather than focus on the end goal, as a group **we focused on the components that increased sales**.

In order to increase up selling of a specific product, I had a monthly contest providing a gift certificate to the employee who up sold the product the most for the month. Only two crew members exceeded the goal. During our monthly financial meeting, **I inquired why only two crew members exceeded the goal**. Coleman stood up and said the incentive was not very motivating. Plus he expressed his desire for the **incentive not to be individual but by team.**

I took his advice and **set up a team contest** for the following month with the winning team going to watch the Dallas Mavericks play (their idea). Coleman's recommendation paid off. The month of the Mavs contest, we **had multiple employees exceed** the desired goal. As promised, the winning team was taken to a Mavs game including food and soft drinks.

Once again the value of listening to my employees paid off. I aligned incentive and rewards based on what was important to them. **When is the last time you asked your employees how they want to be incentivized**? What metrics mean the most to them and why? How should they receive their incentive? By reaching out and listening to your employees, you will be able to devise a plan that will help you drive operational excellence, reward the desired behavior and continue to increase employee engagement. As much as possible, always make sure your employees are part of the decision making process. This will exponentially increase their engagement.

Fact #5 – LET THEM COUNT THE MONEY

Do your employees feel they are empowered to make decisions? If so, will you support their decisions and allow them to learn from their mistakes? Not hold the mistake over their head for days, weeks, months or years? People want to succeed. I do not know of anyone that wakes up and purposely says **"I am going to screw up today"**. It is rare though, when leaders have the right amount of confidence in their employees where they truly empower them to make decisions for the business.

1 – Need to be over or under by $1.00

When you are part of a business, there is nothing more important than the accounts receivable. **Every dollar counts!!!** At the end of the day, it is important to properly count what you made that day. In a fast casual restaurant business, about half your proceeds come from credit card, while the other half is cash receipts. You can imagine with so much cash on hand, there is the potential for some shenanigans. **It is impossible to be in**

multiple places at the same time, hence, you need to empower **your employees and show faith in what they can do.** From my perspective, there is no larger indication of showing faith than allowing someone else to count your money.

Parker was a responsible young man. In fact, when he applied for a job, along with the application, he included a resume. Parker quickly became a top performer and a leader among his peers. With my busy schedule, it was difficult to be as available as I wanted to be. I met with Parker and explained to him how much I appreciated everything he did. In fact, he would now be responsible for counting the accounts receivable at the end of the day. The only caveat was that **WE** could not be $1.00 above or below the cash register report. Parker was concerned he would make a mistake. I assured him after training together for some time, he would be equipped to handle his new challenge.

After my initial meeting and training with Parker, **I kept an eye from afar on his reporting.** There were a handful of occasions where the report differed from the cash register report by $5.00 or so. However, I never had to follow-up with him. On each occasion, he would proactively advise me of the difference and provide an explanation for it. **I purposely stepped back and allowed Parker to make mistakes, grow, learn and own it.** Each time the opportunity presented itself, I would ask his opinion and I would reaffirm my confidence in him. In the two years Parker worked at the stores, the accounts receivable report was "off" a handful of times. However, each instance was properly accounted. By allowing Parker to own his responsibility, I am certain he influenced his peers to make sure they did the right thing every single time.

2 – Hand them the keys

When you own a business, trust has to be far and wide. **You have to trust employees** to open and close your store. Many times, 16-18 year old employees are walking around with the ability to disarm the alarm and enter your store whenever they please. **Without the right level of employee engagement, potentially bad things could happen**.

It was crucial each employee who had a key, understand the responsibility they carried. I recall the first time I handed the keys over to Vince; I asked him if he had ever been responsible for a $100,000 car. Vince's eyes opened widely and he replied with a resounding "No". I responded, "In the store, there is over $100,000 of equipment, furnishing and product, so think about the extent of your responsibility. It's like having the keys to a $100,000 car." **He said "wow".** I reiterated the responsibility that came with the keys, how crucial it was to make sure the store was properly secured and how important it was that he opened and closed the store timely. I also explained to him the vastness of his responsibility. By explaining the **"whys"**, Vince was able to have better regard for the degree of the responsibility he was undertaking.

In reviewing the payroll, I was fascinated by how punctual Vince was in opening the store. Of the hundreds of times he clocked in, he was either early or on time 99% of the time. The other 1%, he was late by no more than a couple of minutes. **I believe this type of commitment came from him being empowered to own his responsibility, having the right level of support and being acknowledged for his continued success.**

3 - #123456789#

The stores' safes could each hold the cash receipts from previous days, customer credit cards that may have been left behind and the beginning days register cash balance. We generally had two cash register drawers in the safe to allow for greater flexibility. Also, **on any given day, there could be thousands of dollars in the safe**. Therefore, those who had access to the safe had to be chosen carefully.

As I mentioned earlier, **career growth is not only about new titles, but additional responsibilities within a current role**. From a business perspective, it was important for the right person to have the safe code. Also, **from an employee engagement perspective**, it was equally as important for the right person to have the safe code.

Having access to the safe was viewed as one of the highest responsibilities in the stores. All employees wanted to be able to access the safe as it was only the elite employees who had that privilege. **Employees who proved their performance over a long period of time were chosen to have access to the safe**. When someone received the safe code, it was a very public statement. I made sure everyone was aware of the announcement, how important the role was within our place and recognized the employee who received such additional responsibility. In addition to publically celebrating the new responsibility, I would privately have a conversation with the employee. The conversation **did not revolve around the additional responsibilities**, the scope or anything to do with the job, but it focused on the value the employee had to the store. **I thanked them for being such a great employee and for being a leader in the store.**

By focusing the conversation on them, how great their performance had been, as well as the trust and faith I had in them, **I never had to discuss the scope of the responsibility**.

This level of acceptance is at the heart of Maslow's top of the pyramid, self-actualization. From my perspective, there is no greater way to improve employee engagement than to empower your employees to handle their task. **The reality is, if you can't fully trust an employee to perform their tasks, then you have the wrong person on the job.**

Sure, there will be some mistakes along the way, but those are learning opportunities. **I have yet to meet anyone that has never made a mistake**. We all have fallen, we all have come short and we all have done things we regret. **However, I would wager each time you fell, you stood back up and learned from your mistake**. If it applies to you, then it should apply to those you lead.

I ask you to provide the same culture you would want for your employees. The satisfaction of knowing you have full autonomy and are able to own the result is the best way to create a self-actualization culture. **Once you have your staff at this level,** the overall engagement of the place will be at a range few have seen or experienced.

Fact #6 – I AM A CREW MEMBER

Do you have the desire to help the front lines? Could you help during an emergency? **Would you be able to roll up your sleeves and stand side by side with your employees?** Regardless of where you are in the chain of command, are you willing and able to get in the middle of the work if, for some reason, you had to do it? If you hesitate for a second to come up with an answer, I can assure you are the cause of poor engagement by your team.

It's not about being functional and knowing how to do every step of the work in great detail. Rather, it's about the culture where **the person that stares at you in the mirror is a human equal to all other humans**. You do not hold yourself above anyone else regardless of your title, position in the company or salary amount. In fact, it should be the opposite, **the higher your degree of responsibility in a corporation, the greater your desire to serve those who work for you**. You are only as good as your weakest link. **The question is, when it comes to employee engagement, are you weakest link?**

1 – What do you want me to do?

There were so many times when I would go into a store and be asked by one of the crew members to help in some way. My immediate question would be, **"What do you want me to do?"** The option was theirs. I could stay in the back, clean and organize or I could go to the front and help with customers. The choice was theirs. I only needed to know how I could help them the most. They knew the need far greater than I did.

I remember receiving a text on Valentine's Day around 9:00 PM from Copeland, stating the store was extremely busy and they needed me to come in to help. **Imagine that, the employee telling the boss what to do.** No, really stop to imagine it. Let me ask you: Are your employees able and willing to openly tell you what is needed?

Since I was not far away from the store, I immediately got in my car and drove to there. **I could have easily said, "No you guys take care of it", "Work harder", "You don't really need me".** I knew when I heard from Copeland, that I was needed. It wasn't up to me to judge the degree of need. I was one of them, **I was a crew member**, and hence, we were all pulling on the rope together.

As soon as I arrived at the store, I could see that the place was terribly busy. I walked into the back where Copeland met me. I asked him, **"Where do you need me?"** He immediately gave me a summary of the night's festivities and instructed me on what was needed. My job for the evening was to stay in the back cleaning, organizing and restocking. **I said OK and started to work as instructed**.

At the end of the day, after all the closing activities had been completed, I asked Copeland if he needed me for anything else. The only two duties that remained were to count the money and close the place. **He responded by saying "We got it now"**. I then left and went home.

It would have been easy for me to simply take over, direct the situation, stay to count the receipts and close the store. **But that was their job. Copeland and Tihuy were responsible that night** to count the receivables and to make sure the store was properly closed. They were in charge that night. **As a leader, I felt comfortable being servant to what they saw best**.

2 – Handle your bis, there I is

I would often say to the shift leaders, assistant managers or managers, **"Handle your bis, there I is"**. The first time anyone would hear it, I would explain **"As a member of our team, you**

are responsible for handling your business, because if not, I will". I am not sure where I got the saying, but it was a fun way to get my message across.

In my opinion, we were all in it together. Hence, we had equal opportunity to provide feedback to one another. **The only requirement was to provide the feedback in a nice way**. I would say, "Pretend you are talking to your grandmother".

I was in the store one Saturday morning visiting with Carlos as he was finalizing the steps before opening. **As Carlos walked to unlock the front door**, the phone rang. I told Carlos I would answer the phone. When I picked up the phone, it was a cake order. I took the cake order form out, went down the form asking the necessary questions, as the customer responded I filled out the form as required.

A week later, I was back at the store. I was in the office looking at different reports, when Raquel came to the back and asked to speak to me. At first, I was wondering what she was going to discuss with me. **Raquel pulled out the order form I had filled out a week earlier**. She asked me if I was the one who had taken the order. I, of course, told her yes. She began to share with me that I had mistakenly written down some of the information incorrectly. Raquel explained to me that the customer was very upset, but she had been able to rectify the situation with the customer. Raquel then turned her attention to me. **She reminded me the importance of properly filling out the form**. In addition, she very politely mentioned that even though she was able to take care of the situation this time, next time she may not be able to do so, which, **in fact, would affect the business**.

I looked at Raquel, smiled a bit and said, "You are right". I apologized for the mistake and told her **I appreciated her feedback**. I further said I would be more careful next time. I later told Raquel how proud I was of her for having the courage to provide me feedback.

I tend to agree with the old saying 'If you talk the talk, you need to walk the walk'. **I couldn't go around telling the employees to handle their business, providing feedback to everyone except me**. If it's good for the goose, it's good for the gander. As a leader/person/crew member I had made a mistake. Raquel had every right to bring it to my attention and hold me accountable.

3 – "Mini J", "H Town", "G"

I have always appreciated leaders who are "real". **Leaders who can be themselves regardless of the situation or circumstance**. I find very few leaders can truly be who they are outside the office in the office. Those who are able to consistently be themselves tend to have a **strong following by their employees**.

Being comfortable in your own skin and not taking yourself to seriously seem to be a good equation for success. One of the fun parts of working in the stores was all the nicknames the employees would give each other. For example, Vince recommended Alvaro. Alvaro was a big kid who was full of laughter and fun. For some reason he acquired the name, "Mini J". I think it was an oxymoron due to Alvaro's size. Similarly, Tihuy had the nickname "H-Town". I heard it was because he was born in Houston.

As one of the crew members, I had been graced with a nickname of my own. One day, I walked into one of the stores. **As I walked in, Carlos said to me "What up G"**. I was not sure he was referring to me, but he was. Later in the day, I asked Carlos, "Where did G come from". He indicated it was the first letter of my given first name. Oh, that made sense. **From that point on, I was known as "G"**.

Every time I walked into a store, I was greeted with "Hey G", "What up G", etc. All the texts started with "G"........ I officially became "G" to all the employees. **It was fitting because I was one of the crew members**.

Who are you as a leader? Are you a leader who will stay in an office, not go out and be one of your employees? Do you mandate, but not participate? **Do your employees really know who you are?** If you answer yes to any of those questions, I can tell you; your team is not fully engaged.

It is difficult to demand respect if you are not willing to give respect. Being one of the employees is easy. **It's about leaving your ego behind.** It's about seeing the world from your employees' perspective. It's about allowing yourself to accept feedback from your employees. It's about wanting to be inclusive and open to others' thoughts. **When employees see you as a person, someone who has weaknesses or someone who is human, you will gain a following from them that will completely blow you away.**

SUMMARY AND ACTION PLANS

As you can tell, employee engagement is not that difficult. But, it does require a commitment from you. By me focusing on these six facts, morale increased, idea generation increased and, most importantly, employee turnover decreased to less than 10%. Keep in mind, in the fast casual restaurant business, employee turnover is typically over 50%. Stop for a second and take that in, half of the employees you hire will leave your company.

In addition, all studies seem to indicate only 3 out of every 10 employees are engaged at work. Other studies indicate 70% of employees are actively looking for a job and approximately 50% of employees do not intend to be with their current employer within the next three years. Imagine all the costs associated with a 50% turnover rate: Training, lost productivity, customer service issues, etc.

Those numbers are staggering. Having to replace 50% of your staff will create challenges beyond belief. But, there is something you can do about it. You can implement the following facts I shared in this book:

1 – **People are People** – Simply put, listen to your employees and treat them the way they expect to be treated (**The Platinum Rule**).

2 – **Know when to hold them, know when to fold them** – Set the right tone and expectations; make sure all employees know how they fit into the big picture. Communicate, communicate, communicate.

3 – **Your mother is from Africa, your dad is in China** – Get to know your employees for the human beings they are. Also, allow your employees to know who you are as a person, not only by what you do at work.

4 – **Gift card, decorate cakes or both** – Find out what motivates your staff and align their strengths to the company's business needs. Take time to develop your employees.

5 – **Let them count the money** – Find ways to empower and support your employees. Provide feedback, encourage risks and forgive mistakes.

6 – **I am a crew member** – Be humble and open to feedback. Focus on being a person, not a title.

The next steps are up to you. It's about taking action. One of the most fascinating things I find about corporate training is the lack of follow-up to ensure that the learning took place. I am not certain how they are able to determine success.

In any case, the table below is a means to allow you to determine how well you are engaging your team. I find it difficult to know if I have learned or grown without first having a baseline. By answering the questions listed in the table below, you will be able to determine how well you are engaging each employee.

Simply answer each question on a scale of 1 to 10, with 1 being the lowest score, where you don't know anything about your employee, and 10 being the highest where you could recite virtually everything about an employee. Then, add all the responses to determine your overall result per employee.

	Employee 1	Employee 2	Employee 3	Employee 4
Is this hire based on their potential?				
Is this employee referring talent?				
Does the employee know how s/he contributes to the bottom line?				
Do you meet with this employee more than once a week?				
Do you know four things outside of work about your employee?				
What type of work does your employee want to do?				
Have you changed a policy based on their feedback?				
Have you empowered this employee to perform their job?				
Have you asked your employee for feedback in the last month?				

Now that you have your result, what does it all mean? The scale below will help you decipher your self-assessment:

10 – 25 – This employee will be resigning within the next few weeks
25 – 40 – This employee will be resigning within the next few months
40 – 60 – This employee will consider another job
60 – 75 – This employee plans to stay the next few months
75 – 100 – This employee plans to stay the next few years

Now that you know where you stand, what do you do next? I would encourage you to focus on questions 2-10. Develop a weekly plan to target the questions for which you had a low rating. For example, if you do not know four things outside of work for a specific employee, on a weekly basis schedule on your calendar to ask that employee something on more of a personal level (HR appropriate).

In the next quarter, take a moment to review your scorecard. Focus on the areas where you have low scores. By targeting each area on a weekly basis you will be able to target each employee. At the end of the 12 weeks, go back to the table and answer each question again. At the very least, you should see an improvement of 25% for each question you have targeted. If you still have some room for improvement, follow the same process and recheck your results the following quarter.

I would also encourage you tell your immediate supervisor and your team that you are working on increasing your engagement score. In addition, ask your supervisor and your employees to hold you accountable for sticking to your plan by having each of them ask you on a quarterly basis to provide them an update on your progress.

Your supervisor/employee/team will serve as your accountability partners. Unless you choose to make a difference and have someone hold you accountable, you will not be able to move the needle on employee engagement. Remember, your success depends on how your team/employee performs. Your team's/employee's success depends on how engaged they are at work. Your team's/employee's engagement depends on how you treat and lead your employees.

As you can see, employee engagement is a vicious circle that starts and ends with you. The success of your team, as well as your success, truly is in your hands. By implementing the 6 facts discussed in this book, you will be able to improve employee engagement beyond your wildest dreams. If you stay true to the course and the 6 facts outlined here, in a few short months your direct reports will have the desire to bring their entire self to work, which will reap countless benefits for the company, for you and most importantly, for all your employees.

About the Author:

Richard Conde is a thoughtful and engaging leader with nearly ten years of experience in senior leadership roles with an advanced degree in management.

Please follow Richard on twitter at @engagethemall for weekly employee engagement tips, comments and highlights. Also, Richard will be providing blogs covering employee engagement topics on www.engagethemall.com